# The Chocolate and Coffee Cookbook

Illustrations by Lillian Langseth-Christensen

# The Chocolate and Coffee Cookbook

Lillian Langseth-Christensen and Carol Sturm Smith

Walker and Company  New York

ISBN 0-8027-2453-1

Library of Congress Catalog Card Number: LC 67-23082

Printed in the United States of America

This Walker Large Print edition published in 1984

# TABLE OF CONTENTS

# HOW TO USE THE BOOK

(1) Read the recipes.

(2) Follow the recipes as exactly as possible. Be particularly careful about instructions concerning the water in the bottom of double boiler: if simmering water is called for, make absolutely certain that the water is not boiling.

(3) Do not open the oven door unnecessarily when baking cakes, but do check before the end of the specified time to see if the cake is done.

(4) Do not open the oven door during the first 20–25 minutes of cooking time for soufflés, as they will fall—and serve the soufflés as soon as they come out of the oven.

(5) When coffee and other beverages are called for, prepare according to your own method or package instructions.

(6) Ingredients in parenthesis are optional.

UNLESS OTHERWISE STATED, ALL RECIPES SERVE SIX. Cake portions depend on the size of the slices.

Chocolate substitutes:

    3 tbs cocoa + 1 tbs butter = 1 square or 1 ounce unsweetened chocolate.
    3 tbs cocoa + 1 tbs butter + 1½ tsp sugar = 1 square or 1 ounce sweet chocolate.

# FRUITS, DESSERTS AND CANDIES

## PEARS HELEN

(1) Cut into 6 large rounds with a large cookie cutter:

*3 slices pound cake*

(2) Place rounds in individual dessert dishes and arrange on them:

*6 canned whole pears*

(3) Melt in the top of a double boiler over hot, not boiling, water and remove from heat:

*2–3 imported\* chocolate bars with raisins, honey, nuts or any combination*

(4) Stir into chocolate and pour the hot sauce over the cold pears:

*½ cup heavy cream*

(5) Serve while chocolate is still hot.

\* Use Tobler, Lindt or Cadbury chocolate, 2–3 bars depending on size.

## PEARS FILLED WITH CHOCOLATE TRUFFLES

(1) Beat until light and thick:

*2 egg yolks*
*½ cup sugar*

(2) Gradually add, then set aside for 30 minutes:

*½ cup powdered sugar*
*1 cup grated chocolate*
*1 tsp vanilla*

(3) Shape into large balls and roll in:

*3 tbs cocoa powder*

(4) Arrange balls in hollows of:

*6 large or 12 small stewed or canned pears, well drained*

(5) Chill and serve on vanilla ice cream or serve plain with soft vanilla ice-cream sauce, page 13.

# APPLE-CHOCOLATE TART

Preheat oven to 350°F before Step 5.

(1) Sprinkle over a buttered 11-inch pie plate and shake to coat evenly:

 ⅓ cup sugar

(2) Line bottom and sides of pie plate with:

 *7 slices slightly stale thin white bread,*
 *buttered on both sides with*
 *½ cup soft butter*

(3) Simmer together over low heat until sugar is melted:

 *6 apples, peeled, cored and sliced very thin*
 *½–⅔ cup sugar, to taste*
 *2 tbs water*
 *grated rind of 1 lemon*

(4) Pour apple mixture over the bread in the pie pan and cover top with:

 *1 cup bread crumbs*
 *½ cup brown sugar*
 *¼ cup grated semisweet chocolate*

(5) Bake until well browned, about 40 minutes. Serve with:

 *1 cup heavy cream, whipped and*
 *sweetened with:*
 *1 tbs powdered sugar*

11

# COFFEE-PRUNE CREAM

(1) Cook prunes according to package directions, but add sugar and use coffee instead of water. Cook until tender:

*2 cups stewing prunes*
*¼ cup sugar, or to taste*
*black coffee to just cover*

(2) Remove prune pits and put prunes through a coarse strainer.

(3) Add to prunes and stir well:

*¼ tsp cinnamon*
*½ tsp instant coffee*

(4) Whip separately until stiff, then fold into prunes:

*2 egg whites*
*1 cup cream, whipped with:*
*powdered sugar to taste*

(5) Mound in glasses, chill and sprinkle over:

*2 tbs grated sweet chocolate*

12

## COFFEE-STEWED PRUNES

(1) Heat to just under boiling:
    *1 1-lb 14-ounce jar prunes, drained*
    *1 cup strong black coffee*
    *1 cup red wine*
    *3 tbs sugar*
    *1 stick cinnamon*
    *1 clove*

(2) Set aside to cool and then chill.

(3) Serve with a topping of:
    *½ cup sour cream, beaten and folded into:*
    *½ cup heavy cream, whipped*

(4) Sprinkle over top:
    *1 tbs sweet chocolate, grated*

## VANILLA ICE-CREAM SAUCE *or* SOFT ICE-CREAM SAUCE

(1) Take from freezer and place in refrigerator for 1 hour:
    *1 quart vanilla ice cream*

(2) Place in mixing bowl and whip until light and foamy:
    *the softened vanilla ice cream*
    *2 tbs rum*

(3) Serve (or fold in before serving:
    *½ cup heavy cream, whipped)*

VARIATIONS: Substitute coffee or chocolate ice cream for vanilla ice cream

## CHOCOLATE CORN FLAKE
## PRALINES

(1) In the top of a double boiler, over hot, not boiling, water, combine and stir until chocolate melts:

2 cups semisweet chocolate chips
6 tbs corn syrup
1 tbs water
2 tsp strong coffee
1 tsp vanilla

(2) Add and stir carefully until chocolate-coated:

1½ cups Corn Flakes
½ cup chopped pecans

(3) Drop by heaping teaspoonsful onto waxed paper and chill until set.

## CHOCOLATE-COCONUT
## PRALINES

(1) Combine and stir over medium heat until mixture comes to a boil, boil *exactly* 1 minute and take from heat:

1½ cups brown sugar, tightly packed
¾ cup coconut
¾ cup chopped blanched almonds
2 tbs instant coffee
2 tbs butter
5 tbs water

(2) Immediately add and stir until melted:

1 cup semisweet chocolate chips
½ tsp vanilla

(3) Drop by heaping teaspoonsful onto waxed paper and chill until set.

## CHOCOLATE POTATOES

(1) Crush with a rolling pin and measure to obtain:

*1½ cups vanilla biscuit crumbs*

(2) Melt over hot, not boiling, water and combine with crumbs:

*2 squares semisweet chocolate*

(3) Add and stir for 10 minutes:

*2 tbs currant jelly*
*2 tbs rum*

(4) Shape* into small potatoes and roll in:

*½ cup chocolate powder or cocoa*

* If dough is too moist to shape well, add biscuit crumbs; if too dry, add a very little heavy cream.

## CHOCOLATE TRUFFLES

(1) Cream butter, then stir in the remaining ingredients in order listed:

*9 tbs butter*
*9 tbs powdered sugar*
*1½ cups unsweetened chocolate, grated*
*1 tbs cocoa*
*3 tbs brandy or rum*

(2) Chill the mixture, then shape into small, uniformly sized balls and roll in:

*¾ cup chocolate nonpareils*

# DOUBLE WALNUT FUDGE SQUARES

(1) Bring to a boil in a heavy saucepan over medium heat and boil 5 minutes, stirring constantly and scraping the bottom of the pan with the spoon:

1¼ cups sugar
⅔ cup evaporated milk

(2) Add and stir until smooth:

¾ cup semisweet chocolate chips
½ tsp vanilla
1 pinch salt

(3) Pour hot fudge into buttered layer cake pan, or pan lined carefully with foil, and cover fudge with:

¾ cup walnut halves or pieces

(4) Set pan in refrigerator. Melt in top of double boiler over hot, not boiling, water and pour over fudge in pan:

¾ cup semisweet chocolate chips
½ tsp vanilla

(5) Chill until set. Cut into pieces and serve on a platter or in paper cases. Depending on size of squares cut, there could be as many as 30–36 pieces.

NOTE: Pecans, raisins or a layer of coconut may be substituted for the walnuts.

# COFFEE BROWNIES

Preheat oven to 350°F.

(1) Sift together and set aside:

> 1 cup flour
> 1 tsp baking powder
> 1 pinch salt

(2) Melt over hot, not boiling, water and set aside:

> ½ cup butter
> 3 squares unsweetened chocolate

(3) In a large bowl, beat eggs, then gradually add remaining ingredients, beating after each addition:

> 3 eggs
> 1⅓ cups sugar
> 1½ tbs instant coffee
> 1 tsp vanilla

> the cooled chocolate, Step 2
> the dry ingredients, Step 1
> ¾ cup chopped pecans

(4) Spread batter in a 7 x 12-inch buttered baking pan and bake 25 minutes. Cool in pan, then cut in squares.

# UNIVERSAL BROWNIES

Preheat oven to 350°F.

(1) Melt over hot, not boiling, water, stir until smooth:

   3½ squares unsweetened chocolate

(2) Cream butter; gradually beat in remaining ingredients in order listed:

   ¾ cup butter
   1½ cups sugar
   3 eggs
   the melted chocolate
   1½ tsp vanilla

(3) Sift together, add nuts and stir into above mixture:

   1 cup and 2 tbs flour
   1 tsp baking powder
   1 pinch salt
   1 cup chopped walnuts

(4) Spread batter in a buttered 7½ x 12-inch baking pan and bake about 30 minutes.

(5) Sprinkle top with powdered sugar or frost with:

   1 recipe hot fudge frosting

(6) When cool, cut into squares. Makes about 48.

# COOKIES, CAKES AND PIES

# CHOCOLATE MERINGUES

Preheat oven to 350°F.

(1) Melt over hot water, do not let water boil, then set aside to cool:
*1 package semisweet chocolate chips*

(2) Beat until half stiff:
*4 egg whites*

(3) Gradually add, while continuing to beat:

*1¼ cups sugar*
*½ tsp vanilla*

(4) Fold into the stiff egg whites:
*the cooled chocolate, stirred until smooth*
*1 cup finely crushed macaroon or*
*cookie crumbs*

(5) Drop or pipe the mixture onto a buttered baking sheet, shaping into rosettes or mounds, and bake until crisp, about 10 minutes. If a second oven is available, dry the meringues at 200°F or "warm" for 15 minutes longer. If only one oven is available, finish baking all meringues, open oven door until oven is cool, then return meringues to dry for 15 minutes.

# FLORENTINES

Preheat oven to 400°F.

(1) Beat together very well:
> 2 whole eggs
> 4 egg whites
> 1⅓ cups sugar
> 1 tsp vanilla
> 1 tsp grated lemon rind

(2) Add and stir well:
> ⅓ cup finely chopped candied orange rind
> 1 tbs finely diced maraschino cherries
> 1½ cups shaved almonds

(3) Sprinkle over and stir in:
> ⅓ cup cake flour
> ½ tsp baking powder

(4) Drop by heaping teaspoonsful onto buttered and floured baking sheet. Spread by pressing on each little mound with a wide knife.

(5) Bake until golden, just about 4 minutes. Lift at once from baking sheet with a spatula and cool.

(6) Spread underside of Florentines with hot chocolate and cool.

## SPREADING CHOCOLATE

(1) In a double boiler over hot water, melt, stirring:
> 1   4-ounce bar German's sweet chocolate

(2) Stir in very slowly, drop by drop:
> 4 drops cooking oil; do not use olive oil

(3) Cool to spreading consistency and use for above. If too dry or if the chocolate dries with a gray color, add 1–2 drops oil and spread while still slightly warm.

# CHOCOLATE-FILLED BULLS EYES

Preheat oven to 350°F.

(1) Cut butter into flour, add sugar and work quickly into a firm dough with hands:

*¾ cup butter*

*1½ cups flour*

*6 tbs sugar*

(2) This dough is hard to handle; roll out a little at a time on a floured pastry cloth with a stocking-covered rolling pin. Cut into fluted rounds and cut a hole in the center of half the rounds.

(3) Bake on a buttered cookie sheet until dry and deep cream colored—do not let cookies actually brown. Take from cookie sheet with a spatula and cool on waxed paper.

(4) Carefully sandwich together with chocolate cream a whole round and a round with a hole in the center. The chocolate cream filling should show through the hole. Handle very carefully, as rounds are fragile. Sprinkle over tops:

*2 tbs powdered sugar, sieved*

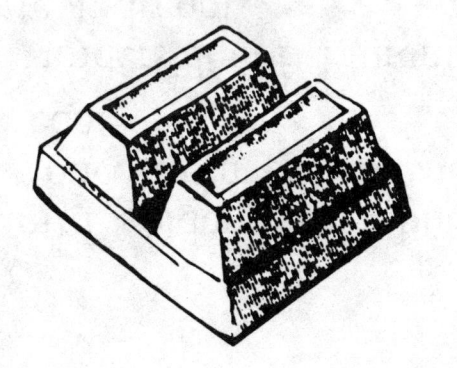

# HALF MOONS

Preheat oven to 375°F.

(1) Sift flour onto pastry board, cut in butter, add other ingredients and work into a smooth dough with hands:

*2 cups and 2 tbs flour*
*¾ cup butter*
*⅓ cup sugar*
*½ tsp vanilla*

(2) Roll dough out thin on a floured pastry board and cut with a crescent cutter. Bake on a buttered baking sheet until dry and lightly browned, about 12–15 minutes, depending on thickness.

(3) Take from baking sheet with a spatula and dip half of each crescent into:

*1 recipe spreading chocolate, page 21*

(4) Arrange on waxed paper to dry, then store in a cool place until needed.

23

# BUTTER ROSETTES

Preheat oven to 350°F.

(1) Cream butter, stir in remaining ingredients in order listed, stirring well after each addition:

> 1¼ cups butter
> ½ cup sugar
> ¼ cup ground almonds
> 2½ cups flour

(2) Pipe dough onto an ungreased baking sheet through a star tube, or any available tube, forming rosettes and rings.

(3) Bake 10 minutes, quickly press into the center of each and continue to bake for 5–10 minutes longer:

> semisweet chocolate chips

# BROWN AND WHITE ROSETTES

Preheat oven to 350°F.

(1) Cream butter and sugar until very light, beat in egg yolks and flour:

1 cup butter
½ cup powdered sugar
4 egg yolks
2½ cups flour

(2) To half the dough add and work in well:

2 tbs cocoa powder

(3) Put plain dough into a cookie press and press rosettes onto a buttered baking sheet. Repeat with cocoa-flavored dough and bake rosettes until golden, about 12–15 minutes. Cool.

(4) Sandwich white and brown rosettes together with chocolate filling.

# COFFEE COOKIES

Preheat oven to 350°F.

(1) Beat yolks until light and creamy, then gradually stir in remaining ingredients in order listed:

6 egg yolks
1⅓ cups sugar
1¼ cups blanched almonds, ground
1 tbs instant coffee
1 tsp vanilla

(2) Beat until stiff and fold into above mixture:

6 egg whites

(3) Drop by heaping teaspoonsful on a buttered baking sheet and bake until crisp and dry, about 25–30 minutes.

# SHARI'S CHOCOLATE CAKE

Preheat oven to 350°F.

(1) Sift, then measure carefully:
> 2 cups cake flour

(2) Sift together 3 times:
> the once-sifted flour
> 2⅔ tsps baking powder
> ¼ tsp salt

(3) Cream butter and gradually add sugar, stirring well:
> ⅔ cup butter
> 1½ cups sugar

(4) Add, one at a time, beating after each addition:
> 3 eggs, beaten individually

(5) Add and blend in well:
> 3 squares unsweetened chocolate, melted
> 1 tsp vanilla

(6) Add alternately, in small amounts, beating until smooth after each addition, beginning and ending with flour:
> ¾ cup milk
> the flour mixture from Step 2

(7) Pour into 2 buttered 9-inch layer pans and bake until a straw tests done, about 45 minutes. Cool thoroughly, fill between layers liberally and use the rest to cover sides and top, piling high:
> 2 cups heavy cream, whipped with:
> 1 tsp vanilla
> 2 tbs sugar

(8) Chill well before serving. The cake will be even better with refrigeration.

# CHOCOLATE CAKE

Preheat oven to 350°F.

(1) Melt in the top of a double boiler over hot, not boiling, water:

> 4 ounces *bitter-sweet chocolate*

(2) Cream in a bowl, then add melted and cooled chocolate and blend well:

> *⅔ cup butter*

(3) Stir in, in order listed:

> *4 egg yolks*
> *2 tbs flour*
> *⅓ cup blanched almonds, finely grated*
> *1 tsp vanilla*

(4) Beat until stiff, then fold in thoroughly:

> *4 egg whites*

(5) Butter, line with paper and butter paper. Pour the batter into a shallow baking pan, 8 x 8 inches and bake about 40 minutes or until a straw tests done.

(6) Cool.

# SEVEN-LAYER CAKE

Preheat oven to 375°F.

(1) With electric beater, cream together:
> 1⅓ cups butter
> 2 cups sugar

(2) Add, one at a time and beat until smooth after each egg is added and before adding the next:
> 5 large eggs

(3) Sift dry ingredients together and add to above mixture, alternating the milk and the flour, beginning and ending with flour:
> 3⅓ cups flour
> 4 tsp baking powder
> ¼ tsp salt
> 1⅓ cups milk, mixed with:
> 1½ tsp vanilla

(4) Butter three 11 x 17 x ¾-inch deep baking pans, line with brown paper, butter the paper and divide the batter evenly among the pans.* Spread tops evenly with a spatula. Bake until golden and until cake shrinks away from sides of the pan and until a straw tests done, about 10 minutes.

(5) Invert cake layers on kitchen towel and draw off brown paper.

(6) Cut 6 perfect 8-inch circles out of cake layers, using a template or plate as a guide and placing it as close to the edge as possible. This leaves three 6-inch wedge-shaped pieces and some scraps. Use the scraps as cake crumbs or ice them for the children. Assemble the three wedges to make a 12-

inch round and cut an 8-inch layer out of them—the filling seals them perfectly into place.

(7) Spread layers with Chocolate Cream Filling, page 33, and ice top and sides with Chocolate Cream Frosting, page 57.

* If only 2 pans are available, do last cake separately in first cooled tin.

# LIL'S INSTANT EASY CHOCOLATE CAKE

Preheat oven to 350°F.

(1) Cream together:
> ¼ cup butter or margarine
> 1 scant cup sugar

(2) Add, one at a time, mixing in well:
> 4 eggs

(3) Add and mix in well:
> 1 can chocolate syrup
> 1 tsp vanilla

(4) Fold in carefully:
> 1 cup sifted self-rising flour

(5) Pour batter into 2 buttered 9-inch round cake pans lined with brown paper, and bake 45 minutes.

# HUNGARIAN CHOCOLATE CHEESE CAKE

Preheat oven to 325°F.

(1) Crush enough rusks with rolling pin to obtain:

　　1½ cups fine Holland Rusk crumbs

(2) Add, stirring well and press onto sides and bottom of well-buttered spring form, then chill:

　　1½ tbs sugar
　　5 tbs melted butter

(3) Melt over hot, not boiling, water, stir well and set aside to cool:

　　2 4-ounce bars German's sweet chocolate
　　½ tsp instant coffee

(4) Beat until light and cream colored, adding sugar gradually:

　　3 eggs
　　¾ cup sugar

(5) Rice cheese through a sieve, then add cream and beat in chocolate mixture, Step 3 and egg mixture, Step 4:

　　3 3-ounce packages cream cheese
　　1¼ cups heavy cream
　　1 tsp vanilla

(6) Sift together and stir into above mixture:

　　5 tbs flour
　　1 pinch baking soda
　　1 pinch salt

(7) Pour into prepared shell, Step 2, and bake about 70 minutes. Cool, chill and serve with heavy or whipped and sweetened cream.

# DOBOS TORTE

This is the distinguished Hungarian ancestor of our Seven-Layer Cake.

Preheat oven to 375°F.

(1) Beat until cream colored and thick:

8 egg yolks
⅔ cup sugar

(2) Sift together, then beat into yolk mixture:

⅔ cup flour
¼ tsp salt

(3) Beat until stiff, then fold into batter:

8 egg whites

(4) Work with as many 9-inch cake pans as you own. Turn them upside down, butter the outside bottom and on each stick a 9-inch round of brown paper. Butter the paper well, dust with flour, and spread ⅐ of the cake batter on the paper with a spatula.

Do not let edges get thinner than the center. Bake 2 at a time for about 7 minutes, or until crisp and cream colored.

(5) Loosen paper from pan and cool cake layers on paper. Re-prepare pans and continue until seven layers are completed.

(6) Insert knife between paper and cake and draw off paper carefully. Turn layers upside down and use, smooth side up.

(7) Select the smoothest layer and glaze it with a clear sugar glaze. Spread other layers evenly with chocolate cream filling and assemble the torte with the sugar-glazed layer on top. Spread sides of cake with chocolate filling and pipe rosettes of chocolate filling around the edge of the top, placing one on each portion. Center the rosettes with:

12 blanched and toasted hazelnuts or
filberts, unsalted

## CHOCOLATE CREAM FILLING FOR LAYERS AND SIDES OF DOBOS TORTE AND LAYERS OF SEVEN-LAYER CAKE

(1) Combine in the top of a double boiler over hot water until chocolate is melted, stirring, then set aside:

6 squares semisweet chocolate

3 tbs boiling coffee

(2) Rinse out top of double boiler and in it beat:

6 eggs

¾ cup sugar

(3) Set top of double boiler over simmering water in bottom half and stir egg mixture until thick, about 10 minutes.

(4) Take from heat, pour into a cold bowl and gradually beat in the melted and cooled chocolate. Beat slowly until cool, then beat in until smooth:

1 cup and 3 tbs soft butter

½ tsp vanilla

(5) Refrigerate until just cold enough to spread perfectly.

## SUGAR GLAZE FOR TOP LAYER

(1) Melt in a heavy pan over medium heat until clear and golden:

¾ cup granulated sugar

(2) Pour it, all at once, onto the center of the top layer of the cake and tilt the layer in such a way that the glaze spreads over all of it. If necessary, help to spread the glaze with a long knife. Work quickly. When top is covered, dip knife in oil and mark off 12 even divisions, cutting down through the glaze. After the glaze is cold it will splinter when cake is cut, so the cuts must be made before the glaze has set.

# BISHOP'S BREAD

Preheat oven to 300°F.

(1) Beat together until light and creamy:
   6 egg yolks
   ⅔ cup sugar

(2) Add gradually and stir in well:
   1 cup flour

(3) Add and stir in well:
   ¾ cup almonds, scalded and sliced
   ½ cup white raisins
   ½ cup dark raisins
   (½ cup chopped citron)
   2 cups semisweet chocolate chips

(4) Fold in, pour into buttered and floured loaf pan and bake 1 hour:
   6 egg whites, stiffly beaten

Serve in thin slices. This tastes even better after 24 hours.

34

# ICE CREAM ON CHOCOLATE ROUNDS

Preheat oven to 350°F.

(1) Melt over hot, not boiling, water, stir well and cool:

    2 squares unsweetened chocolate
    6 tbs soft butter

(2) Sift together and set aside:

    ⅔ cup flour
    ½ tsp baking powder
    1 pinch salt

(3) Beat well, gradually adding ingredients in order listed:

    2 eggs
    1 cup sugar
    1 tsp vanilla
    the chocolate mixture from Step 1

    the sifted flour mixture from Step 2
    ⅔ cup chopped walnuts or pecans

(4) Pour mixture into buttered muffin tins, filling them about half full and bake for about 20 minutes. In standard muffin tins this makes about 12 rounds.

(5) Top rounds with scoops of vanilla ice cream or sandwich 2 rounds together with ice cream in between. For added richness, serve with a hot chocolate sauce.

# CHOCOLATE ROLL

Preheat oven to 375°F.

(1) Beat together until thick:
   1 cup powdered sugar, sifted
   6 egg yolks
   2½ tbs cocoa powder

(2) Beat until stiff and fold in:
   6 egg whites

(3) Pour into a flat buttered 11 × 17 × ¾-inch pan and bake until a straw tests done, about 10–15 minutes.

(4) Turn out on waxed paper, cover with waxed paper, cool slightly but roll while still warm.

(5) Whip together until stiff:
   1 pint heavy cream

   sugar to taste
   1 tsp vanilla

(6) Unroll chocolate roll, remove paper, fill ½-inch thick with whipped cream and roll again.

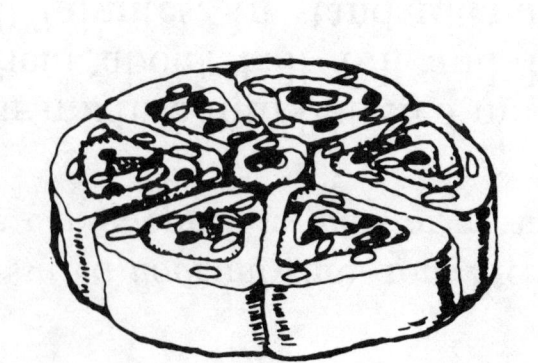

# COFFEE WALNUT ROLL

Preheat oven to 375°F.

(1) Beat yolks and sugar until thick and cream colored, then stir in remaining ingredients:

6 egg yolks
⅔ cup sugar
1 tbs instant coffee
1½ cups finely chopped or ground walnuts
1 tsp baking powder
1 tsp vanilla

(2) Whip egg whites half stiff, gradually add sugar, while beating until stiff, then fold into above batter:

6 egg whites
2 tbs sugar

(3) Butter an 11 x 17-inch cookie pan, line with brown or waxed paper and butter paper. Add the batter, spread evenly with a spatula and bake until a straw tests done, about 15 minutes.

(4) Let roll cool 5 minutes, invert carefully on a kitchen towel sprinkled with powdered sugar and draw off paper.

(5) As soon as roll is cold, spread with:

2 cups sweetened heavy cream, whipped or
1 recipe Kaffeeklatsch Cream, page 85

(6) Lift edge of towel at both ends and start rolling cake up into a long, narrow roll.

(7) Sprinkle with:

2 tsp powdered sugar, sieved

# CHOCOLATE CHESTNUT CAKE TOURINOISE

Preheat oven to 400°F.

(1) Cut a cross on the flat side of:
>    *2 lbs large chestnuts*

(2) Roast in the oven on a cookie sheet until the shells spring open and are easily pulled off, about 12 minutes. If the inner shell comes off too, all the better.

(3) In a saucepan, boil chestnuts for about 7 minutes, drain and draw off remaining inner skin.

(4) Set a glass or metal loaf pan into freezer of refrigerator to chill.

(5) Return chestnuts to saucepan and boil 30 minutes in:
>    *water to cover*
>    *¼ tsp salt*

(6) Press chestnuts through a strainer or potato ricer and stir in:
>    *¾ cup sugar*
>    *½ cup soft butter*
>    *1 tsp vanilla*
>    *1 tbs brandy*

(7) Melt over hot, not boiling, water, then combine with chestnuts:
>    *8 ounces semisweet chocolate*

(8) Pour the mixture into the chilled mold and return to refrigerator until set, about 2 hours.

(9) Unmold and serve decorated with:
>    *1 cup heavy cream, whipped*

38

# PIE CRUSTS

## A FLAKY PASTRY CRUST

Enough for two 9-inch double-crust pies

(1)  Sift into a bowl:
>  4 cups sifted flour
>  1 tsp salt

(2)  Cut in with a pastry cutter until completely distributed:
>  1 cup lard or ½ cup lard and
>  ½ cup vegetable shortening

(3)  Sprinkle over dough, stir until it gathers, then gather with hands, roll into waxed paper and chill:
>  4½–5 tbs ice water

## CHOCOLATE PIE CRUST

(1)  Sift into a bowl:
>  1⅓ cups flour
>  ½ tsp salt
>  ¼ cup sugar
>  ¼ cup cocoa powder

(2)  Cut in until evenly distributed:
>  7 tbs shortening or butter

(3)  Sprinkle over:
>  ½ tsp vanilla mixed with:
>  4–5 tbs ice water

(4)  Stir with a fork until dough gathers, then gather with hands, roll into a ball, wrap in waxed paper and chill.

39

## GRAHAM CRACKER CRUMB CRUST

Combine and press mixture onto bottom and sides of a 9-inch pie pan, but do not make a high rim:

1⅔ cups graham cracker crumbs, about 28 crackers

5 tbs granulated sugar

5 tbs soft butter

¼ tsp vanilla

## WALNUT CRUMB CRUST

Preheat oven to 300°F.

Combine and press mixture onto bottom and sides of a 9-inch pie pan without making a high rim and bake about 10 minutes, then cool before filling:

1 cup finely crushed graham cracker crumbs, about 16 crackers

½ cup finely chopped walnuts

6 tbs firmly packed brown sugar

6 tbs melted butter

## COCONUT CHOCOLATE PIE SHELL / FOR CREAM OR ICE-CREAM PIES

(1) In a heavy pan, melt over low heat, stirring constantly:

*3 squares unsweetened chocolate*
*3 tbs butter*

(2) In a bowl, stir, then add melted chocolate and stir until smooth:

*1 cup confectioners' sugar*
*3 tbs hot milk*

(3) Add and stir well:

*2¾ cups flaked coconut*

(4) Spread mixture over bottom and sides of an 11-inch pie pan and chill until set.

(5) Fill with coffee or vanilla cream or ice-cream filling. If ice cream is preferred, fill shell with small scoops of coffee ice cream and sprinkle with grated chocolate. Serve ice-cream-filled pies at once.

41

# COFFEE CREAM PIE

Preheat oven to 400°F.

(1) In the top of a double boiler combine and bring to a boil over direct heat, stirring constantly:

> 2 cups heavy cream
> 1½ cups strong coffee
> ¾ cup sugar
> 6 tbs flour
> 3 tbs cornstarch
> 2 tbs instant coffee

(2) Set over boiling water, in lower section of double boiler and cook, stirring, until thickened, about 5 minutes. Set aside.

(3) In a small bowl, beat until thick and creamy:

> 9 egg yolks

(4) Beat a little of the coffee cream into the yolks, then reverse and slowly beat the yolk mixture into the coffee cream.

(5) Set again over boiling water and cook, stirring constantly, for about 3 minutes. Pour into a chilled bowl and stir until cold. Fold in *half* of:

> 1 cup heavy cream, whipped

(6) Pour the coffee cream into the following pie shell, cover top with reserved cookies and pipe a large rosette of the remaining whipped cream on each cookie and on the center of the pie.

# SUGAR DOUGH FOR PIE CRUST AND HEART-SHAPED COOKIES

(1) Sift onto a pastry board and make a well in the center of:

> 3 cups flour

(2) In the well put:

> ½ cup sugar
> 6 egg yolks
> 1 pinch salt

(3) Over the well slice:

> ¾ cup butter

(4) With hands, work the butter and yolks into the flour to obtain a smooth dough. If too dry, add a little heavy cream.

(5) Chill dough, then roll out thin—about ⅛-inch—and use to line one 11-inch pie plate. Flute edge. Reroll remaining dough and cut into 7 or 8 heart-shaped cookies.

Fill shell with raw rice and bake until golden, about 12–15 minutes. Remove rice. Bake cookies on buttered cookie sheet for about 7 minutes or until golden. Cool shell and cookies before using.

# CHOCOLATE-TOPPED COFFEE PIE

(1) Fill a 9-inch pie pan with one of the pie crusts, pages 39–43. If a baked crust is chosen, bake and cool. Fill the shell with the following filling.

(2) Stir together and set aside to soften:

> 2 tbs cold coffee
> 1 tbs cold milk
> 1 tsp rum
> 1 envelope gelatin

(3) In top of a double boiler, stir well:

> 6 tbs sugar
> 2 egg yolks
> 1¼ cups scalded milk
> 2 tsp instant coffee
> ½ tsp vanilla

(4) Set over simmering water and stir well until smooth and slightly thickened. Take from heat and stir in the gelatin mixture. Chill.

(5) Whip until stiff, adding the sugar gradually:

> 2 egg whites
> 6 tbs sugar

(6) Whip and fold into stiff egg whites:

> 1 cup heavy cream

(7) Beat cold coffee mixture of Steps 3 and 4, fold in combined egg whites and whipped cream and fill into pie shell.

(8) Melt in top of double boiler over hot, not boiling, water; remove from heat:

> ¾ cup semisweet chocolate chips
> 1 tbs butter

(9) Beat in until smooth, then pour in a thin stream over chilled pie, making a criss-cross design over the entire surface and chill until needed:

> 1 tbs hot coffee

44

# CHOCOLATE CREAM PIE

Preheat oven to 350°F.

(1) Heat in the top of a double boiler over hot, not boiling, water until chocolate is melted, then set aside in a bowl to cool:

>3 squares unsweetened chocolate
>1¾ cups milk

(2) Combine in the top of the double boiler:

>1 cup sugar
>4 tbs flour
>1½ tbs cornstarch
>1 pinch salt

(3) Gradually stir in, place over boiling water and cook, stirring constantly, until thickened and smooth, about 7 minutes:

>the cooled chocolate milk
>4 egg yolks, beaten

>1½ tbs butter
>1 tsp vanilla

(4) Add, cool and pour into a 9-inch pie shell:

>1 tsp vanilla

(5) Combine and whip until half stiff:

>4 egg whites
>¼ tsp cream of tartar
>1 pinch salt

(6) Gradually add to egg whites and continue whipping until stiff:

>7 tbs powdered sugar

(7) Spread some of the egg whites along the edge of the pie filling, then heap the remainder high in the center. Bake until lightly browned, about 14 minutes.

# THREE-LAYER COFFEE BISQUIT TORTE

Preheat oven to 375°F before baking.

(1) In an electric mixer, cream butter, add sugar slowly and beat until thick and cream colored:

> 3 tbs sweet butter
> ⅔ cup sugar

(2) Add one at a time, beating after each addition:

> 8 egg yolks
> 4 tsp instant coffee
> 3 tbs heavy cream

(3) Add gradually, continuing to beat:

> 1⅓ cups flour

(4) Whip until half stiff:

> 8 egg whites

(5) Continue to whip while gradually adding:

> 2 tbs sugar

(6) Fold stiff egg whites into egg yolk mixture, Step 3, and pour batter into 3 cake pans, 9 inches wide, buttered, lined with paper, buttered again and floured.

(7) Bake until lightly browned and a straw tests done, about 20–22 minutes. Invert on cake racks and cool.

(8) Fill with Coffee Butter Cream and ice with Chocolate Cream Frosting. This is a dry, crisp layer cake, so spread heavily with filling.

## MOCHA FILLING FOR TORTE

(1) Melt over hot, not boiling, water, stir and set aside to cool:

*4 squares unsweetened chocolate*

(2) In top of double boiler beat until light and creamy:

*7 eggs*
*1 cup and 3 tbs sugar*

(3) Place over simmering water in lower section of double boiler and cook, stirring constantly, until thickened, about 10 minutes.

(4) Take from heat, pour into a chilled bowl and beat in cooled chocolate and:

*1 cup unsalted butter*

(5) Chill for a short time to harden slightly before spreading on layers and sides of torte.

# FILLINGS, FROSTINGS AND SAUCES

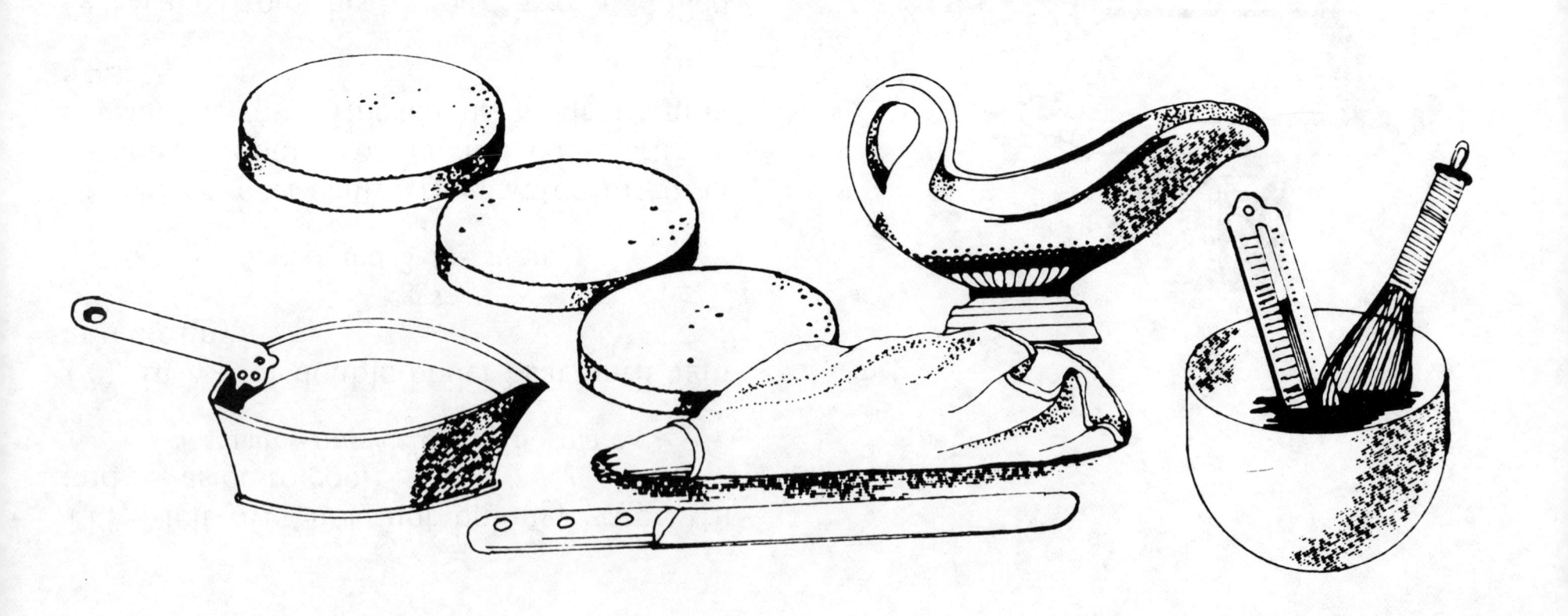

# CHOCOLATE WAFFLES

(1) Sift together:
>> 1½ cups flour
>> 1½ tsp baking powder
>> ½ tsp salt

(2) Melt in the top of a double boiler over hot, not boiling, water. Stir until smooth and take from heat:
>> 1½ packages semisweet chocolate chips or
>> 9 ounces
>> ½ cup butter
>> ¾ cup milk
>> ½ tsp vanilla

(3) Beat together until light, then gradually add above mixture:
>> 3 eggs
>> ¾ cup sugar

(4) Beat above mixture into the sifted flour mixture of Step 1. (If batter is too stiff, beat in:
>> 2–3 tbs milk)

(5) Heat ungreased waffle iron, fill half full with batter and bake as for regular waffle.

(6) Serve hot with:
>> 1 pint soft coffee ice cream

MAKES ABOUT 6–7 WAFFLES

Preheat oven to 350°F.

(1) Boil in a small, heavy pan until butter is melted:

> 1 stick butter
> 1 cup water

(2) Add, all at once, and stir until mixture becomes dry and leaves the side of the pan:

> 1 cup flour

(3) Take from heat and beat in:

> 1 tbs sugar
> 1 egg

(4) When the egg has been completely incorporated, beat in, one after the other, incorporating each before the next is added:

> 3 eggs

(5) Drop the batter by the heaping tea-spoon* onto a buttered baking sheet and bake until puffed, brown and dry, about 40 minutes. Cool puffs before filling them.

(6) Whip and pipe into the puffs through a small hole cut in the bottom:

> 1½ cups heavy cream
> 3 tbs sugar

(7) (Or, slit puffs and fill with tiny scoops of chocolate or vanilla ice cream.)

(8) Chill puffs immediately.

(9) Before serving, melt in the top of a double boiler over hot, not boiling, water:

> 4 ounces unsweetened chocolate
> ¼ cup butter
> 1⅔ cups sugar

(10) Beat in until smooth:

50

*1 cup heavy cream*
*1 tbs rum*

(11) Serve in individual dishes and pour hot chocolate sauce over each portion.

* To facilitate dropping batter, use 2 spoons and dip them in hot water before scooping up the dough.


## COFFEE SAUCE FOR CREAM PUFFS FILLED WITH CHOCOLATE ICE CREAM

(1) In top of double boiler, over simmering water, heat until sugar is dissolved:
*¾ cup milk*
*2 tbs instant coffee*
*¼ cup sugar*

(2) In a bowl, beat and then add above mixture in a very thin stream, beating constantly:
*4 egg yolks*

(3) Return mixture to top of double boiler and cook, stirring constantly, until thickened, about 10 minutes.

(4) Pour mixture into a chilled bowl, add, stir in and chill:
*1 tsp vanilla*
*(½ tsp coffee essence)*

(5) Before serving, fold in:
*1 cup heavy cream, whipped*
*1 egg white, beaten until stiff*

(6) Sprinkle over top:
*2 tbs grated chocolate*

# CHOCOLATE PANCAKES

Preheat oven to 200°F.

(1) Beat together in order listed until smooth, then chill 1 hour:

3 eggs
3 egg yolks
1½ cups water
1½ cups sifted flour
1 tsp baking powder

(2) Beat batter again with:

¼ cup heavy cream

(3) Batter should be the consistency of heavy cream, add additional heavy cream if necessary.

(4) Pour 2 tbs batter into each of 2 buttered 8-inch pancake pans, which will make 6-inch pancakes, and tilt pans to cook the pancakes evenly. Cook until lightly browned over medium heat, turn to brown second side and repeat until all the batter is used up. Brush pans with butter between each pancake and keep finished pancakes warm in the oven in a covered casserole, or folded into a warm kitchen napkin. Allow the first pancake to begin cooking slightly before starting with the second pan to allow enough time to keep the two pans going without burning either of them.

# PANCAKE FILLINGS AND TOPPINGS

(I) Fill each pancake with 2–3 tbs chocolate pudding prepared from a mix and sprinkle tops with sieved powdered sugar.

(II) Fill each pancake with 2–3 tbs vanilla pudding prepared from a mix and sprinkle tops with 1 tsp grated chocolate.

(III) Center on each pancake a 6 x 1-inch slice of hard vanilla ice cream and sprinkle tops with 1 tsp grated bitter chocolate.

(IV) Center on each pancake a 6 x 1-inch slice of hard chocolate ice cream and garnish with a zigzag stripe of melted chocolate.

# BUTTER CREAM FILLING

(1) Stir together in the top of a double boiler over steam* until creamy and warm, then remove from heat:

    2 whole eggs
    3 egg yolks
    1¼ cups sugar

(2) Add and beat until cold:

    2 tbs instant coffee
    1 tbs brandy

(3) Soften, beat until creamy and combine well with above mixture:

    1¼ cups butter

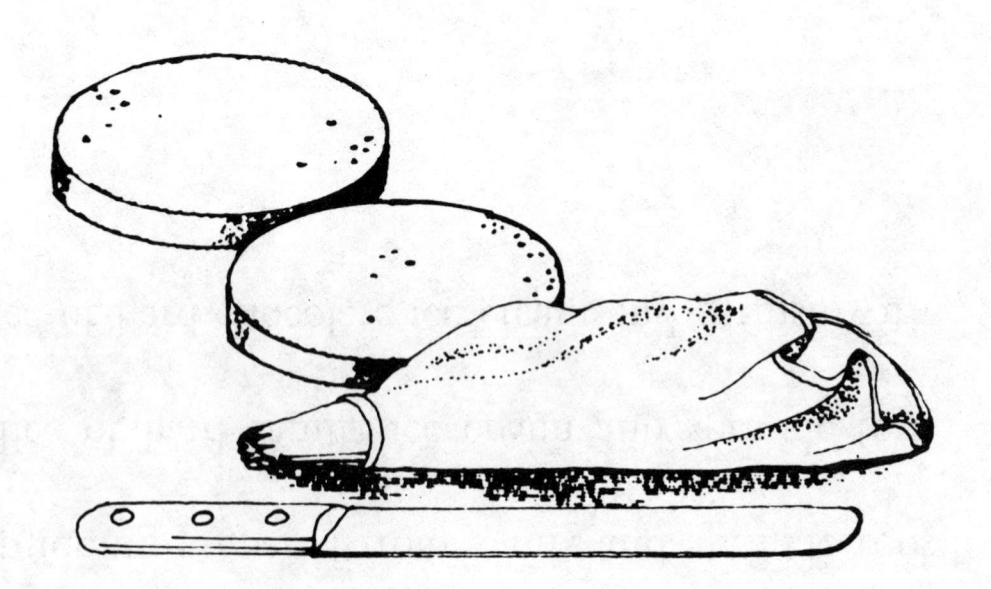

* Boiling water should not touch upper section of double boiler.

# COFFEE BUTTER CREAM

(1)  Into mixer bowl sift together:
2½ cups powdered sugar
3 tbs cocoa
3 tbs instant coffee
1 pinch salt

(2)  Gradually beat in but do not overbeat:
½ cup soft butter
4 tbs heavy cream
1 tsp vanilla

(3) Add more soft butter and cream, to taste, keeping in mind that filling will harden when chilled:
½ cup soft butter
2 tbs heavy cream

(4) Spread cake layers and top with butter cream, fill remaining cream into pastry bag and pipe around edge of cake through a fluted tube.

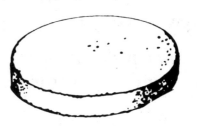

## COFFEE BUTTER CREAM TOPPING
## AND FILLING / FOR CAKES AND TORTEN

(1) Heat cream, stir in coffee until dissolved:

> ¼ cup heavy cream
> ¼ cup instant coffee

(2) Beat in, alternatingly, but do not overbeat:

> 1¼ cups soft butter
> 2 cups sifted confectioners' sugar

(3) Add and beat until smooth:

> 2 egg whites
> 1 tsp vanilla
> 1 cup sifted confectioners' sugar

(4) Depending on thickness desired, increase confectioners' sugar to taste.

(5) Spread filling generously on 3 layers and sides of plain or mocha cake, and sprinkle sides with:

> 1½ cups cookie crumbs or
> finely chopped nuts

(6) Decorate top of cake with crisscross lines and a border of butter cream.

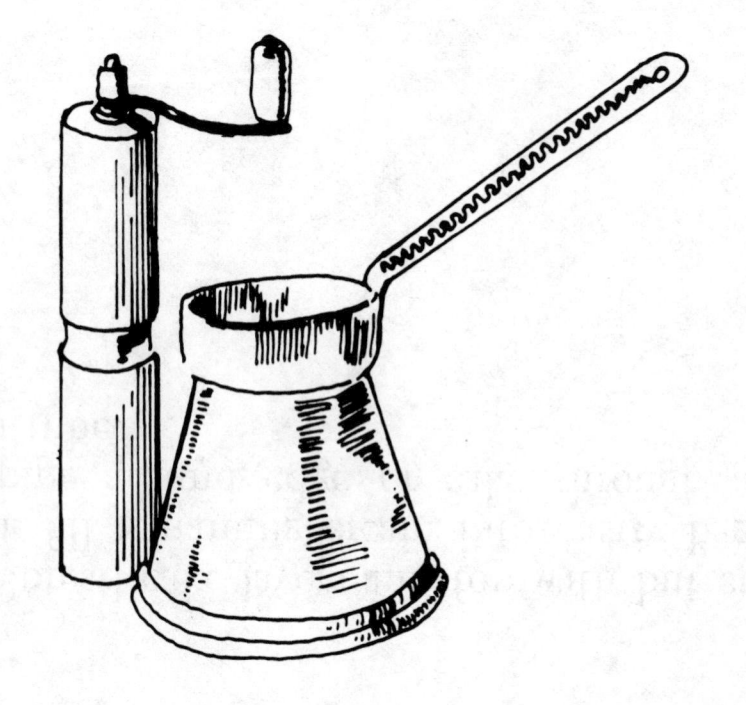

56

# CHOCOLATE CREAM FROSTING

(1) Cream butter, gradually add remaining ingredients, in order listed, and stir until light:

> 1 cup and 3 tbs soft butter
> ¾ cup sugar
> 1 tbs cocoa powder
> ½ tsp vanilla
> (½ tsp coffee essence)
> 1 pinch salt

(2) With electric beater, beat until light and creamy, then add above mixture and beat until smooth:

> 3 eggs
> ¾ cup sugar

(3) Use to frost a 2-layer, 9-inch cake between the layers and outside. Press choco-late nonpareils or finely chopped nuts against the sides.

# HOT FUDGE FROSTING

(1) Cook over medium heat, stirring constantly, until sugar and chocolate are dissolved:

> 1½ cups brown sugar
> 1½ cups granulated sugar
> 3 squares unsweetened chocolate,
>   cut into pieces
> ¾ cup milk or evaporated milk

(2) Continue to cook, stirring constantly, until the mixture forms a soft ball when a little is dropped and tested in cold water—238°F on a candy thermometer.

(3) Take from heat and beat in until proper spreading consistency is reached:

> 1 tbs sweet butter
> 2 tsp vanilla
> 1 pinch salt

(4) Spread on cake. If frosting becomes too thick to spread, set over warm water and stir in a little more milk or evaporated milk. Refrigerate cake before serving.

58

## CHOCOLATE FROSTING AND FILLING

(1) Melt in top of double boiler over hot, not boiling, water, beating with a hand beater, then cool:

8 ounces semisweet chocolate
½ cup strong black coffee
½ cup water

(2) Cream butter, gradually add sugar and eggs and beat until light:

1½ cups butter
1½ cups sugar
4 egg yolks
1 tsp vanilla

(3) Beat chocolate mixture into above mixture and chill to spreading consistency.

(4) Spread between cake layers and sides and top of cake.

## CHOCOLATE-COVERED FRUITS / A GARNISH FOR DESSERTS

(1) Melt in top of double boiler over hot, not boiling, water, stirring constantly:

1 package semisweet chocolate chips

(2) Let chocolate cool but do not chill. When the chocolate is at room temperature, dip into it, holding fruit by stems:

12 large strawberries, thoroughly dried
12 small clusters seedless grapes, thoroughly dried
12 pieces candied orange peel

## CHOCOLATE DOLLARS / FOR TOPS OF PIES, CAKES, MOUSSES AND CREAMS

(1) Melt in top of double boiler over hot, not boiling, water:

    *½ lb German's sweet chocolate*

(2) Take from heat and set aside to cool, but *do not* chill.

(3) Draw about 24 circles on waxed paper; use the bottom of a glass or a cup. The circles should not be more than 3 inches in diameter.

(4) Spread a thin layer of the cooled chocolate on each circle with a knife. Chill until needed. Draw off paper and store leftover Dollars in refrigerator.

## CHOCOLATE SAUCE I

(1) In the top of a double boiler, melt over hot, not boiling, water:

    *4 squares semisweet chocolate*
    *¼ cup sugar*
    *½ cup heavy cream*
    *¾ cup coffee*

(2) When chocolate is melted, beat until smooth, take from heat, cool and then beat in:

    *¼ cup heavy cream, or to taste*
    *½ tsp vanilla*
    *½ pinch cinnamon*

Serve hot or cold.

60

## CHOCOLATE SAUCE II

(1) Melt in heavy saucepan over very low heat, stirring constantly:
>    4 squares unsweetened chocolate
>    1 cup heavy cream

(2) Take from heat and stir in:
>    1½ cups sugar
>    ⅓ cup butter
>    1 tbs instant coffee

(3) Return to low heat and cook, stirring constantly, for 4 minutes, then beat in and serve hot or cold:
>    1 tsp vanilla
>    1 tbs rum

## MOCHA SAUCE

(1) Combine and stir until marshmallows are dissolved:
>    2 cups boiling coffee
>    1 package tiny marshmallows

(2) Beat the mixture until smooth and chill.

(3) Before serving, fold into the coffee mixture:
>    1 cup heavy cream, whipped

(4) Serve sauce over boiled chestnuts, vanilla, coffee or chocolate ice cream or sponge-cake fingers.

# FUDGE SAUCE

(1) Cook until chocolate is melted, stirring constantly:

 2½ squares semisweet chocolate
 2½ cups sugar
 1 cup light cream
 2½ tbs light corn syrup
 1 pinch salt

(2) Continue to cook, stirring constantly, until mixture forms a soft ball when a little is tested in cold water—234°F on a candy thermometer.

(3) Take from heat and add, but *do not stir*, then set aside until lukewarm:

 2½ tbs butter
 1 tsp instant coffee
 1 tsp vanilla

(4) When lukewarm, beat mixture in a beater or with a wooden spoon until creamy. Then add a little at a time until desired consistency is reached:

 ¼–½ cup heavy cream

(5) Before serving, reheat in top of double boiler over boiling water.

62

## CHOCOLATE ORANGE SAUCE
## FOR VANILLA ICE CREAM

(1)  Melt over low heat, stirring constantly:
2 4-ounce bars German's sweet chocolate
½ cup heavy cream
2 tbs strained orange juice
2 tbs curaçao or other orange liqueur

(2)  Add and cook, stirring constantly, until sugar is dissolved and sauce thickens very slightly:

1 cup sugar
1 pinch salt

(3)  Take from heat, cool slightly, beat in and serve:

6 tbs butter
½ tsp vanilla

63

# HOT AND COLD DESSERTS

# COFFEE BISQUIT TORTONI

(1)  Heat and stir until smooth, then cool:
*½ cup heavy cream*
*3 tbs instant coffee*

(2)  Whip until stiff:
*2 egg whites*

(3)  Add to whites and whip 3 minutes longer:
*½ cup sugar*
*the cold coffee-cream*

(4)  Whip until stiff:
*2 cups heavy cream*

(5)  Fold into whipped cream:
*the egg white mixture*
*1 cup crushed* **macar**oon *crumbs*
*3 tbs sherry*

(6)  Fill mixture into 6 ramekins or baking cups and sprinkle with:
*⅓ cup crushed macaroon crumbs*

(7)  Place in freezer or freezing compartment for 2 hours. Take out and place in refrigerator at least 15 minutes before serving.

## VIENNESE ICED COFFEE DESSERT

(1) Have ready:
6 cups strong, unsweetened iced coffee
1 cup heavy cream, whipped
1 cup almond crunch candy,
crushed or chopped
1 pint hard-frozen vanilla ice cream,
in round container

(2) Set out 6 glasses of approximately the same diameter as the ice cream container.

(3) Pour 1 cup iced coffee into each glass, cover completely with 1 slice of the hard-frozen ice cream, about 1 inch thick. Pipe or mound the whipped cream on the ice cream and sprinkle the crunch candy over the whipped cream.

## COFFEE ZABAGLIONE

(1) Beat with an electric hand beater in the top of a double boiler over simmering water until the mixture thickens and rises:
6 egg yolks
6 tbs sugar
1 cup strong black coffee
¼ tsp vanilla

(2) Serve at once in stemmed glasses.

# GRANDMOTHER'S CHOCOLATE ICE CREAM

For hand-turned or electric ice-cream freezer

(1) Melt in top of double boiler, over simmering water, stirring constantly:

3 squares unsweetened chocolate
2 cups milk
¾ cup sugar
1 pinch salt
1 tsp instant coffee

(2) Beat in a bowl until light:

4 egg yolks
4 tbs sugar

(3) In a thin stream, stir a little of chocolate mixture 1 into egg yolk mixture 2. Then reverse and gradually pour egg yolks into chocolate and cook, stirring constantly for 2 minutes. Set aside until cold.

(4) Stir in and pour into chilled freezer container:

2 cups heavy cream
1 tsp vanilla
1 tsp coffee essence

(5) Adjust container pack with:

8 parts ice to:
1 part salt

(6) Turn until stiff, take out paddle, pack sealed container in ice and salt or put it in freezer for 3 hours.

# CHOCOLATE BOMBE

(1) Invert a rinsed 1½-quart bombe mold, a rounded cone-shaped mold, place it in a saucepan to hold it upright and line the entire surface with:

*1 quart coffee ice cream*

(2) Using a flat ice-cream packer or strong kitchen spoon dipped in warm water, smooth the ice cream up the sides of the mold leaving a deep well in the center.

(3) Chill the lined mold in freezer or freezing compartment while preparing the Chocolate Bombe mixture.

(4) Melt in a heavy saucepan over low heat, stirring constantly:

*2 squares unsweetened chocolate*
*2 tbs rum*
*2 tbs milk*

(5) Add and continue to stir for 3 minutes:

*½ cup sugar*
*1 pinch salt*

(6) Stir chocolate mixture gradually into yolks, then cool:

*2 egg yolks, beaten*

(7) Whip cream until softly stiff, then fold into chocolate mixture and pour into well in mold:

*2 cups heavy cream*

(8) Freeze for at least 2 hours in freezer. Dip mold into hot water, invert on a serving platter and unmold.

# MOLDED CHOCOLATE RING

(1) Stir together and set aside:
>  1 envelope gelatin
>  ¼ cup cold coffee
>  1 tsp vanilla

(2) Stir together in the top of a double boiler over hot, not boiling, water until melted:
>  1 4-ounce bar German's sweet chocolate
>  ¼ cup sugar
>  1 cup heavy cream
>  ¾ cup milk
>  1 pinch salt

(3) In a small bowl, beat lightly:
>  3 egg yolks
>  3 tbs sugar

(4) In a thin stream, stir a little of the chocolate mixture of Step 2 into the yolk mixture. Then reverse and gradually stir the yolks into the chocolate. Reduce heat to low and cook, stirring, until lightly thickened. Take from heat and stir in gelatin mixture of Step 1 until dissolved.

(5) Place in refrigerator until cold, but before the edges begin to set, fold in:
>  3 egg whites, beaten stiff with:
>  5 tbs powdered sugar
>  1 cup heavy cream, whipped

(6) Pour mixture into rinsed ring mold and chill until set, at least 2 hours.

(7) Loosen top edge with knife, dip mold into hot water and invert on a serving platter. (OR: Hold serving platter over mold, invert and shake lightly onto platter.)

(8) Fill center with whipped cream, beaten vanilla ice cream or fruit.

69

# COFFEE BAVARIAN CREAM

(1) Combine, stir and set aside to soften:

    *2 envelopes gelatin*
    *½ cup cold coffee*

(2) In the top of a double boiler over boiling water, stir until hot:

    *1 cup confectioners' sugar*
    *1 cup milk*
    *2 tbs instant coffee*

(3) Take from heat, add gelatin and stir until dissolved. Cool. When mixture is cold but before it starts to set, beat it well and fold in:

    *2 egg whites, beaten stiff*
    *2 cups heavy cream, whipped*
    *1 tbs rum*

(4) Pour mixture into a 2-quart oiled mold and put in the coldest part of the refrigerator until set, at least 2–3 hours. Do not freeze.

(5) Serve with sweetened whipped cream.

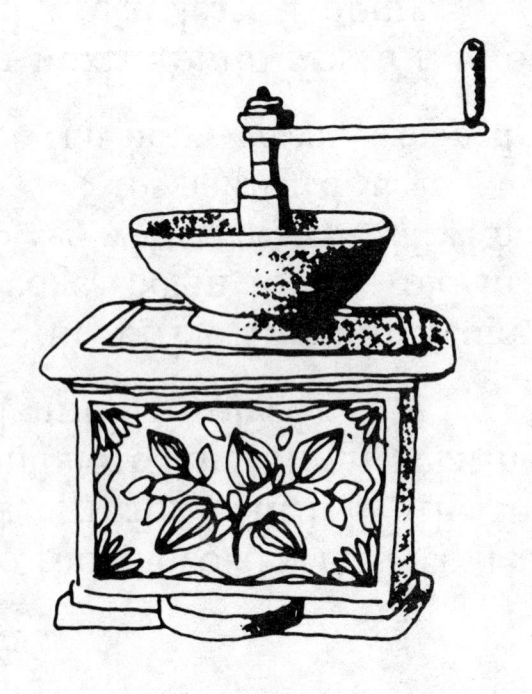

# CHOCOLATE LADYFINGER CAKE

(1) Cream until light and set aside:
  ½ cup butter
  ½ cup sugar

(2) Combine and beat well:
  1 egg
  ½ cup milk, scalded and cooled

(3) Melt over hot, not boiling, water, beat until smooth, then stir into above mixture and cool:
  8 ounces semisweet chocolate
  1 tbs rum or water

(4) Stir cooled chocolate mixture into mixture of Step 1 until smooth.

(5) Arrange in a soufflé dish a layer of ladyfingers, cover with chocolate mixture, continue with a second layer of each, then sprinkle with nuts:
  2 packages ladyfingers, separated and cut to fill corners of dish
  ½ cup chopped walnuts or pecans

(6) Refrigerate for at least 2 hours.

# FRENCH POTS OF CHOCOLATE CREAM / POT DE CRÊME

(1) Combine in the top of a double boiler over hot, not boiling, water until melted, stirring well:

    1 4-ounce bar German's sweet chocolate
        1½ cups heavy cream
          3 tbs sugar

(2) In a small bowl beat only long enough to combine:

      6 egg yolks
      2 tbs sugar
      ½ pinch salt

(3) In a very thin stream, stir a little of the chocolate mixture, Step 1, into the yolk mixture, Step 2. Then reverse and stir the yolk mixture, very gradually, into the chocolate. When all is added, continue to stir, over hot water, until smooth and thickened, about 7 minutes.

(4) Take from heat and stir in:

      1 tsp vanilla

(5) Pour chocolate cream into 6 little French "pots" or custard cups and chill at least 2 hours before serving.

# FRENCH CHOCOLATE MOUSSE I

(1) Melt in a double boiler over hot, not boiling, water, stirring. Remove from heat and cool:

> 3 squares unsweetened chocolate

(2) Beat, adding sugar gradually, until very light and thick:

> 4 egg yolks
> ⅔ cup sugar

(3) Add cooled chocolate to above yolk mixture.

(4) Beat until half stiff, start adding sugar gradually and continue to beat until stiff:

> 4 egg whites
> ¼ cup powdered sugar

(5) Fold whites into chocolate mixture and add, folding in:

> 1½ cups heavy cream, whipped

(6) Pour mixture into 1½-quart bowl or 6 individual cups and chill at least 4 hours before serving with heavy cream.

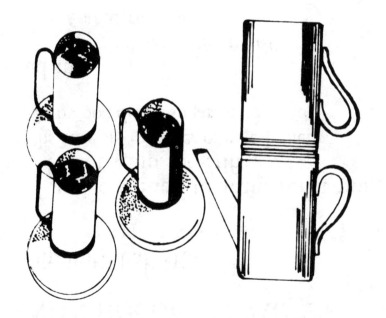

## FRENCH CHOCOLATE MOUSSE II

(1) Melt over hot, not boiling, water then stir until smooth and cool:

*6 ounces semisweet chocolate*

*3 tbs rum*

*3 tbs black coffee*

(2) Beat well until light and creamy, then add to chocolate mixture:

*6 egg yolks*

*¾ cup sugar*

(3) Whip until stiff and fold into chocolate mixture:

*6 egg whites*

(4) Pour mousse into a crystal dish and cool, but do not chill until last 30 minutes before serving.

(5) Sprinkle over top and serve:

*½ cup chopped walnuts*

## FROZEN MOUSSE WITH ORANGES AND CHOCOLATE SAUCE

(1) Whip until half stiff:

*1½ cups heavy cream*

(2) Add and continue to whip for a minute, but do not whip too stiff:

*3 tbs curaçao or other orange liqueur*

*3 tbs powdered sugar or to taste*

(3) Fold in:

*3 egg whites, beaten stiff*

*grated rind of 1 orange*

(4) Pour mixture into a rinsed ring mold and place in freezer or freezer compartment for 4 hours.

(5) Unmold and fill center with:

*6 peeled and pitted oranges, sliced across*

(6) Serve with a Chocolate Sauce, page 60.

# FROZEN CHOCOLATE MOUSSE

(1) In a heavy saucepan, over very low heat, melt, stirring constantly:

> 2 squares unsweetened chocolate
> 2 tbs strong coffee

(2) Add, increase heat to simmer and cook, stirring constantly, for 3 minutes, then take from heat:

> 5 tbs sugar
> 1 pinch salt

(3) In a small bowl, beat until creamy:

> 2 egg yolks
> 4 tbs sugar
> ½ tsp vanilla

(4) In a very thin stream, stir a little of the chocolate mixture into yolk mixture, then reverse process and stir the yolk mixture very gradually into the chocolate. Set aside until cold.

(5) Whip until stiff, then fold into chocolate mixture:

> 1½ cups heavy cream

(6) Pour into a 1-quart mold or 6 individual oiled molds and freeze in a freezer for at least 3 hours.

# FROZEN CHOCOLATE SOUFFLÉ

(1) Fold a piece of waxed paper in half, lengthwise, and tie it around the outside of a ¾-quart straight-sided baking dish or dish suitable for serving. A 2-inch cuff should extend above the top rim of the dish. Place in the refrigerator until needed.

(2) Stir together in a small bowl and set aside for 10 minutes:

*2 envelopes gelatin*
*¼ cup rum or sherry*

(3) Melt in top of double boiler over boiling water, stirring constantly, pour into a cold bowl and beat until smooth and cooled, about 2 minutes:

*5  1-ounce squares semisweet chocolate*
*the softened gelatin*
*⅔ cup milk*

(4) Beat in the top of double boiler over simmering water until very thick and creamy, about 6 minutes:

*5 egg yolks*
*⅔ cup sugar*

(5) Remove egg yolk mixture from heat, beat until cool, about 4 minutes, then stir in:

*1 tsp vanilla*
*the cooled chocolate mixture*

(6) Whip separately until stiff and fold into above mixture before gelatin begins to set:
*1½ cups heavy cream*
*5 egg whites*

(7) Pour into prepared dish and chill at least 4 hours. Remove paper cuff before serving. Use a warm knife blade if it sticks. Sprinkle over and serve:

*1 tbs powdered sugar*

# CHOCOLATE ALMOND SOUFFLÉ

Preheat oven to 375°F.

(1)  Cook over low heat, stirring constantly, until chocolate is melted, then set aside:

2 squares unsweetened chocolate
¾ cup sugar
2 tbs rum
1 tsp vanilla
1 pinch salt

(2)  In a heavy saucepan, over low heat, stir butter and flour together until smooth, then gradually stir in milk until smooth and thickened:

3 tbs melted butter
3 tbs flour
1 cup milk

(3)  Combine above mixtures, cook over low heat, stirring constantly, for 3 minutes. Take from heat, cool and add:

4 egg yolks, beaten until creamy
1 cup ground scalded almonds

(4)  Beat until stiff, then fold into cooled soufflé mixture:

6 egg whites

(5)  Pour into buttered 2-quart soufflé dish and set dish in a shallow pan of hot water. Bake in oven for 1 hour.

(6)  Serve with sweetened whipped cream, softened ice cream or chocolate sauce.

# CHOCOLATE SOUFFLÉ

Preheat oven to 375°F.

(1) Stir together well in the top of a double boiler, off the heat:

> 6 egg yolks
> ¾ cup sugar

(2) Add, little by little, and continue to stir until smooth:

> ½ cup cake flour

(3) Add, place over simmering water and stir for 1 minute:

> 2 cups milk

(4) Add, continue to stir until the chocolate is melted and the mixture is thick, then remove from heat:

> 4 squares chocolate

(5) Beat until very stiff, allow to rest for 10 minutes and beat again:

> 8 egg whites

(6) Add to cooled mixture:

> 2 tsp real vanilla

(7) Fold the egg whites into the mixture carefully, pour into a buttered and floured 2-quart soufflé dish and bake 30 minutes for a runny soufflé or 35 minutes for a soufflé with a soft core.

(8) Serve with a sauce made by folding in or stirring together:

> 1 pint soft vanilla ice cream
> ½ pint heavy cream, whipped

# MOCHA SOUFFLÉ

Preheat oven to 375°F.

(1) In a heavy saucepan, combine over low heat:

> 3 tbs melted butter
> 4 tbs flour

(2) Stir in gradually and continue to stir until thickened, then take from heat:

> 1 cup milk

(3) Beat together until light, then stir into milk mixture:

> 5 egg yolks
> ½ cup sugar
> 3 tbs instant coffee, or to taste
> 2 tbs dark rum
> 1 pinch salt

(4) Beat until stiff, then fold into above mixture:

> 6 egg whites

(5) Pour mixture into an ungreased soufflé dish, set into a shallow pan of water and transfer the two into preheated oven. Bake 35 minutes for a soft, creamy soufflé and 45–50 minutes for a medium dry soufflé.

(6) Serve with a softened ice cream sauce of:

> ½ pint heavy cream, whipped and
> folded into:
> 1 pint soft coffee ice cream

# COFFEE CASSEROLE

Preheat oven to 325°F.

(1) Melt butter over low heat and stir in remaining ingredients until smooth:

> 4½ tbs butter
> 6 tbs flour
> ½ cup sugar
> 1 tbs cocoa
> 3 tbs instant coffee

(2) Stir in gradually and cook, stirring constantly, until thickened and smooth:

> 1½ cups milk

(3) Remove from heat and stir in:

> 6 egg yolks, well beaten
> 1 pinch salt
> 1 tsp vanilla

(4) Fold in, pour into a 2½-quart casserole and bake for 1 hour:

> 8 egg whites, beaten stiff

(5) Serve with soft vanilla ice cream.

## QUICK BAKED ALASKA

Preheat oven to 375°F.

(1) Carefully enlarge center opening of cake and fill the opening with ice cream. Place on a heatproof platter and refrigerate:

1 angel food cake

1½ pints coffee or chocolate ice cream

(2) Beat until very stiff and spread on sides and top of cake:

6 egg whites

1 pinch salt

⅓ cup sugar

(3) Make swirls on top and smooth the sides with a knife, dust over and bake until meringue is lightly browned, 3–5 minutes; watch carefully:

⅓ cup sugar

(4) Serve immediately.

## CHOCOLATE CASSEROLE PUDDING

Preheat oven to 375°F.

(1) Melt over hot, not boiling, water in the top of a double boiler, stirring:

1½ cups semisweet chocolate chips

(2) Remove from heat, beat until smooth, add and stir in well:

1½ cups ground almonds

¾ cup sugar

1 tsp vanilla

6 egg yolks

6 tbs diced candied fruit

(3) Fold in carefully and bake in a 2-quart casserole for 45 minutes:

6 egg whites, stiffly beaten

(4) Serve with a soft coffee ice-cream sauce.

# CHOCOLATE PUDDING

Preheat oven to 350°F.

(1) Sift together into a bowl:
  1½ cups flour
  3 tsp baking powder
  1 cup sugar

(2) Add to flour and stir in well:
  ½ cup grated chocolate
  ¾ cup milk
  ¾ cup chopped pecans
  3 tbs melted butter
  1 tsp vanilla
  1½ tsp instant coffee

(3) Pour into a buttered 2-quart casserole and top evenly with a mixture of:
  ¾ cup brown sugar
  ¼ cup sugar
  5 tbs grated chocolate
  ½ tsp vanilla

(4) Pour over ingredients in casserole and bake 1 hour:
  1½ cups boiling water

(5) Pudding will form its own sauce. Serve hot with sweetened whipped cream to taste.

# BEVERAGES

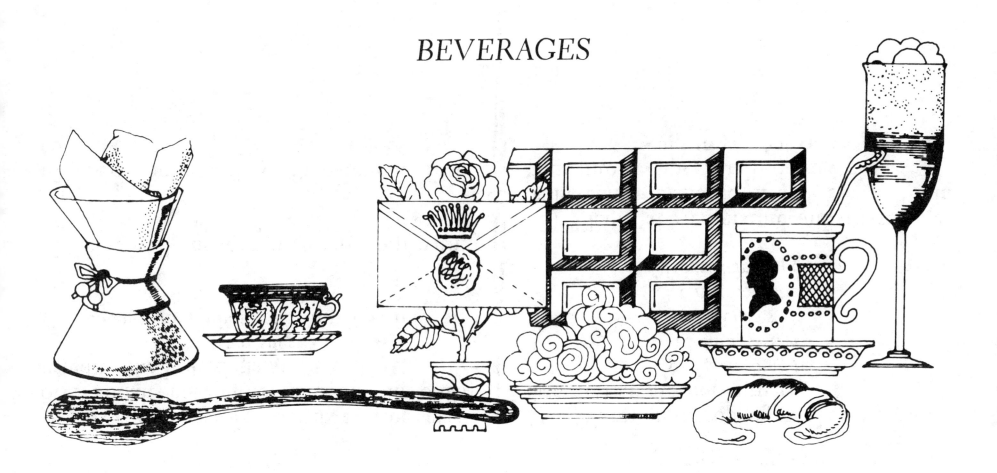

## IRISH COFFEE

(1) *For each person.* Heat a wine glass over an alcohol burner and add in order listed to the heated glass:

2 tsp sugar
enough strong hot coffee to fill ⅔ full
3 tbs Irish whiskey

(2) Stir well and carefully cover top with:
whipped cream

(3) Serve immediately. Prepare one Irish coffee at a time.

## CAFÉ BRULOT

(1) Warm in a copper pan or heatproof dish over an alcohol burner:

6 jiggers brandy
12 lumps sugar
8 cloves
3 cinnamon sticks
1 curl lemon peel

(2) Flame above mixture and as soon as flame starts to die down add, stir well and pour into 6 cups or tall, narrow glasses:

5 cups strong, hot coffee

## FRENCH COFFEE

(1) Rub sugar cubes over orange rind until they pick up flavor from the orange:

> 6 lumps sugar
> 1 eating orange

(2) Combine in a saucepan and heat until sugar is melted:

> the sugar from Step 1
> 6 cloves
> 1 cinnamon stick
> 1 cup rum

(3) Add, bring to a boil and serve immediately:

> 5 cups hot coffee

## KAFFEEKLATSCH CREAM FOR COFFEE

(1) Two hours before guests arrive, combine and stir until perfectly smooth, then chill:

> 3 tbs powdered sugar
> 2 tbs instant coffee
> (½ tsp coffee essence)
> ½ tsp vanilla
> 1 dash cinnamon
> 1½ cups heavy cream

(2) When guests arrive, put on coffee and just before serving whip the cream mixture until stiff. Mound it in a chilled bowl and spoon generously onto large cups of hot coffee just as they are being served.

## SWISS COFFEE

(1) Divide over 6 cups:
*6 chocolate "kisses" or small pieces*
*of milk chocolate*

(2) Pour over chocolate and serve with hot milk and sugar passed separately:
*6 cups hot coffee*

## JAMAICAN COFFEE

*For each person. Heat a wine glass and add sugar as above. Fill only ½ full with strong, hot coffee and add enough warmed rum to almost fill glass. Stir and add whipped cream to cover the entire surface, as above. Serve immediately.*

## RUSSIAN COFFEE I

(1) Divide over 6 heavy cups:
*6 lumps sugar*

(2) Divide over sugar in cups:
*⅔ cup warmed vodka*

(3) Flame the vodka until sugar dissolves, then divide over cups and serve:
*6 cups strong, hot coffee*

## RUSSIAN COFFEE II

Combine in a saucepan, bring to a boil and serve immediately in mugs or large cups and pass sugar separately:
*3 cups strong coffee*
*3 cups red wine*
*1½ cups vodka*
*sugar to taste*

86

## CAFÉ DIABLE

(1) Warm in a heatproof pan over an alcohol flame until the smell of roasting coffee can be detected:

> 12 coffee beans

(2) Add and heat, but do not boil—if coffee beans are omitted, begin this step over the burner:

> 6 cloves
> 1 cinnamon stick
> 1 dash vanilla
> 1 curl orange rind
> 1 curl lemon rind
> 3 jiggers brandy
> 2 jiggers Benedictine or 2 jiggers brandy

(3) Flame mixture, add to extinguish flames and strain into cups:

> 5 cups strong, hot coffee

87

## HOT SHERRIED COFFEE I

(1) Combine and pour into 6 cups:

> 3 cups hot chocolate, prepared with milk
> 3 cups hot coffee
> 1 pinch salt

(2) Add to each cup and serve with sugar passed separately:

> 1–1½ tsp sherry

## HOT SHERRIED COFFEE II

(1) Prepare as above, but add sugar to taste before proceeding.

(2) Divide cream over cups and sieve the cocoa over the cream:

> ¾ cup heavy cream, whipped
> 3 tsp cocoa powder

## HOT BRANDIED CHOCOLATE

(1)  Prepare according to package directions:

    *6 cups hot chocolate*

(2)  Add, stir until coffee is dissolved and pour into cups:

    *2 tbs instant coffee*
    *2 tbs brandy, or to taste*
    *sugar to taste*

(3)  Sprinkle over and pass sugar separately:

    *grated nutmeg*

## HOT COCOA-COFFEE WITH ALMONDS

(1)  Prepare with water according to package directions:

    *3 cups cocoa*

(2)  Combine with cocoa and heat, but do not boil:

    *3 cups hot coffee*
    *1 dash almond extract*
    *sugar to taste*

(3)  Serve in cups sprinkled with:

    *⅓ cup finely chopped scalded almonds*

## HOT MIDNIGHT COFFEE

(1) Place in each of 6 cups:
   1/8 tsp ground cinnamon, or to taste
   1/2 tsp cocoa powder
   1 tsp brandy
   sugar to taste

(2) Fill into cups and stir well:
   6 cups hot black coffee

## HOT CAPUCCINO

(1) Divide over 6 large cups or glasses to fill each 3/4 full:
   4 1/2 cups strong, hot coffee
   sugar to taste

(2) Divide over glasses to fill each to brim:
   1 cup heavy cream, half whipped

(3) Divide over top of cream in each glass:
   3 tsp cocoa powder
   1 1/2 tsp grated orange rind

## JAMAICAN JAVA, COLD

Combine ingredients well, pour into tall, ice-filled glasses and pass sugar separately:

1½ cups iced cocoa, prepared with water
1½ cups strong, iced coffee
1½ cups chilled heavy cream
1½ cups light rum
(sugar to taste)

## ALEXANDER COFFEE, COLD

Per serving. Place in each wine glass:
2 tbs crème de cacao
fill with strong iced coffee
top with 2 heaping tbs sweetened
whipped cream

## ICED CHOCOLATE COFFEE I

Beat or blend all ingredients and serve in tall glasses:

3 cups strong, iced coffee
6 tbs chocolate syrup
3 cups coffee ice cream

## ICED CHOCOLATE COFFEE II, WITH RUM

(1) Beat or blend together well:
2 cups strong iced coffee
4 cups chocolate ice cream
½ cup dark rum, or to taste

(2) Serve in tall glasses, sprinkled with:
¼ cup chopped walnuts

## ICED COCOA-COFFEE MILK

(1) Boil together for 3 minutes, remove from heat and set aside 4 minutes to cool:

> 3 tbs granulated sugar
> 3 tbs cocoa
> ¾ cup coffee

(2) Add and chill well:

> 3 cups cold milk
> 1 cup cold cream

(3) Pour into tall glasses filled with cubes and serve:

> 2 trays coffee ice cubes*

\* Strong black coffee frozen into cubes in ice cube tray.

## ICED COFFEE WITH KIRSCH

Per serving. (1) Fill each glass half full with chopped ice and add:

> 2 tsp fast-dissolving sugar
> ½ jigger kirsch

(2) Fill glasses with:

> strong iced coffee

(3) Top with:

> whipped cream
> chocolate shavings

## ICED VANILLA CHOCOLATE AND COFFEE

(1) Combine and pour into chilled glasses:
   3 cups iced chocolate
   3 cups iced coffee

(2) Divide over glasses and sprinkle with chocolate:
   1 cup vanilla ice cream, slightly softened
   and whipped or beaten until light
   3 tbs grated chocolate

## SHERRIED ICED CHOCOLATE

(1) Combine and chill:
   4 cups hot chocolate, prepared according
   to package directions
   1 cup strong hot coffee
   1 cup dry sherry

(2) Just before serving, pour into 6 tall glasses and top with:
   ⅔ cup heavy cream, half whipped

92

# CHOCOLATE AND COFFEE WITH MEAT DISHES

The use of chocolate and coffee to flavor and enhance meat dishes is a limited practice, but there are a few very famous dishes that should be mentioned. Perhaps the most famous is the Mexican Turkey Mole, an elaborate dish with a list of many, many ingredients, including peppers, pumpkin seeds and Mexican chocolate. Chicken Mole is often available in many Mexican restaurants.

The use of coffee with meat dishes is more common, and a leg of lamb roasted in coffee or with a coffee sauce stands high on the list. There are many ways of using the coffee with lamb —some cooks use coffee already sweetened and with milk or cream added, others use black coffee. We like to marinate the leg of lamb in coffee for a few hours before roasting and before inserting garlic slivers into the meat. If the leg of lamb is to be dredged in flour, add instant coffee to the flour for dredging. Use the coffee marinade for basting during the last hour of cooking, and make your sauce from the pan drippings as usual.

Coffee can also be added to chopped meat, barbecue sauces and pork dishes. If the meat to be prepared calls for additional liquid, use prepared coffee, if not, use instant coffee. Do some experimenting—the coffee is used more as an accent than as a strong flavor. Like the use of a bay leaf in stews, it should be sensed rather than actually tasted. One particularly good coffee recipe is:

93

# HAM STEAK WITH PEACHES

(1) Cook in a heavy pan with no additional fat—or use two pans and divide ingredients equally between the pans—over medium heat until browned on both sides:

*6 round ham slices, about 8 ounces each,*
*½ inch thick*

(2) Pour over ham slices, increase heat and boil until the sauce has bubbled up and wrapped itself around the meat and almost but not quite evaporated, about 7–8 minutes:

*1½ cups orange juice*
*juice of 3 lemons*
*½ cup loosely packed brown sugar*
*2 tbs instant coffee*

(3) Remove ham slices and keep warm. Add and cook quickly in glaze remaining in pan only until well covered with the glaze and heated through:

*12 canned peach halves, well drained*

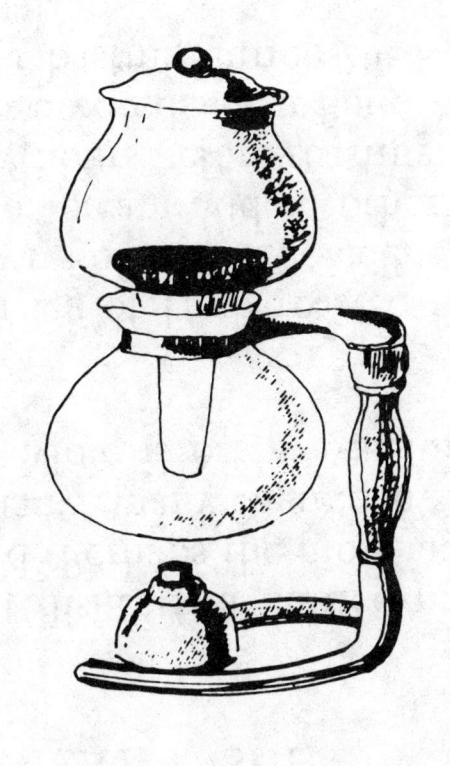